Why Is It Not Me?

Olamma Maji

A catalogue record for this book is available from the National Library of Australia

Copyright © 2021 Olamma Maji
All rights reserved.
ISBN: 978-1-922343-73-4

Linellen Press
265 Boomerang Road
Oldbury, Western Australia
www.linellenpress.com.au

Dedication

I dedicate this book to anyone
who is experiencing a delay
in what they wish for.

Contents

Dedication iii

Contents v

Introduction - Why me? 1

Chapter One - Why is it not me? 3

Chapter Two 6

Chapter Three - The battle of the mind 11

Chapter Four 14

Do not forget 16

Do not forget 17

Chapter Five - What to do 19

About the Author 22

Introduction

Why me?

Often people ask questions like, why me? When something bad happens to them, they say, why am I going through what I am going through?

Why is this happening to me?

Why do I have this cancer?

Why this disease?

Why can't I have children like others?

Why is the queen of England not my mother?

Why is my relationship not working out?

Why was I born in this country where there is poverty?

Why is God not answering my prayers?

Why is he allowing this to happen to me? I am a nice person; I am good to people; I serve God, and I am faithful in my giving. I have been obedient to his word; I am committed to his work … why do I have to go through what I am going through? Why do I have to struggle this much to live, to survive?

Why me? Why! Why! Why!!!?

Almost everyone at some point in their lives has asked the question: why me?

Prophet Elijah in the Bible complained as well. He said he was not better than his fathers, that God should take his life when he heard Jezebel was looking for him to kill. (1 Kings 19:4) That was a question of why me? Why must I go through this Lord? All I did was to serve you. He felt the worst had happened to him. Just like Prophet Elijah, some people seek to take their life because of what they are going through.

Chapter One

Why is it not me?

The focus of this book is to try and answer the question people often ask, especially believers. When I say believers, I mean those who have accepted the Lord Jesus as their personal saviour – those who are born again. The question 'why is it not me?' is asked when something good happens to someone else, especially if you are desiring that same thing.

Believers often go through battles in their minds. They get upset, and get angry with God sometimes. This affects their prayer life; affects their relationship with God, and some end up backsliding when they see others getting what they've been struggling to get for years, without knowing how long it took that person to get that thing, without knowing how long they struggled, waited, prayed, and fasted. Furthermore, without knowing the process it took the person to arrive at their destination, they get upset with the person, upset with God and upset with life in general.

They often ask, 'Why am I not the one with the gift of healing? Why is my ministry not growing like Mr B's? Why can't I prophesy? Why am I not seeing visions like Mr B? Why is this happening to Mr B and not me? Why! Why!! Why!

I remember what happened to me after I finished high school years ago. I was, to the best of my knowledge, one of the smartest students in the class. I sat in the very first row during classwork with our teachers. I was serious and very committed to my studies. I never missed school; never missed a class. The teachers praised me for my punctuality, tenacity, and devotion towards my school work. Furthermore, I was very obedient at home, making sure my house chores were attended to after school. After graduating from high school, it took four years of waiting to get into university, due to the competitive nature of the few available admission spaces and the grades needed to occupy those spots.

Despite all my efforts, admission into the university did not come through for me at that time. So, whenever I came across my high school mates, they often asked what university was I studying at. I felt really bad because I was still trying to get in while some of them were almost graduating from their university of choice. I cried a lot and asked myself, "Why is it not me? Why am I not in the university?" After all, I did all that I was supposed to do: I was a good girl; I wore a long dress or skirt; I styled my hair as required; I was obedient; I served God. So why should those who were disobedient to teachers and never attended classes frequently be in the university while I was at home for four painful years, waiting.

It hurt me so bad that I contemplated suicide but could not do it because I knew it was a sin to take one's life.

Most times, believers pray and fast to manifest a particular gift. They go to church frequently; they feel they are very serious but the gift is just not coming through. Then they see another believer who does not look serious, who does not go to church as often as they do, who does not even pray much, manifesting that same gift they desire. They start asking God, 'Why is it not me?'

This battle of questioning resides more in the mind; they cannot tell anyone what they are thinking or what they are going through because they don't want to feel judged.

Chapter Two

When the Lord instructed Samuel to anoint for him a king after he had rejected Saul as king over Israel, Samuel went to the house of Jesse. When Samuel looked at Eliab, the first son of Jesse, he was so sure that he was the one to be anointed as king because of his build. But God told Samuel not to look at his physical appearance because he had refused him. Jesse called Aminadab, his second son, and made him pass before Samuel. The Lord still said no, he was not the chosen one. Seven of Jesse's children passed before Samuel, and still the Lord said no, they were not the chosen ones.

"and Samuel said to Jesse are all the young men here? then he said there remain yet the youngest and there he is keeping the sheep and Samuel said to Jesse send and bring him, for we will not sit down till he comes here" (1 Samuel 16:11).

"then Samuel took the horn of oil and anointed him before his brothers."

(1 Samuel 16:13).

You can imagine the number of 'Why is it not me?'s David's brothers would have accumulated on their minds. The first-born Eliab would have asked 'Why didn't the Lord choose me? After all, I am the first child; I am strong, tall, well built; I have fought for my country. Why did the Lord choose my little brother who has not been to war?

David's brothers would have asked what they did wrong, what could their brother have that they didn't have, although they were stronger than him. These questions would have been running through their minds. To make matters worse, Samuel instructed Jesse and his sons not to sit until David arrived, which shows the urgency and seriousness of the situation. Oil was used to anoint David King by Prophet Samuel in the presence of his brothers, who were not allowed to sit until his arrival. That must really have hurt their feelings.

"and in the process of time, it came to pass that Cain brought an offering of the fruit of the ground to the Lord, Abel also brought of the first born of his flock and of their fat, and the lord Respected Abel and his offering but he did not respect Cain and his offering and Cain was very angry and his countenance fell" (Genesis 4:3-5) *"now Cain talked with Abel his brother and it came to pass when they were in the field that Cain rose up against Abel his brother and killed."* (Genesis 4:8)

The Lord accepted the offering of Abel but rejected that of Cain. This did not make sense to Cain; the question of 'Why is it not me?' came up there. Why did the Lord not accept his offering but accepted his brothers? Cain must have asked within himself what he might have done wrong. He must have used phrases like: that was not fair; why is not mine accepted? Cain could not handle the question, so he killed his brother.

Like Cain, some people have killed their brothers or sisters, either physically or spiritually with words, because they could not handle the question 'why is it not me?'

Some people speak ill of those who have been successful; they lay false accusations to ruin their reputation, in effect killing them in the eyes of others. Just because a man of God is gifted in a way they are not, they say he uses charm, voodoo, juju, and make further comments like, 'he is fake', 'it is not God', 'it is witchcraft or the power of the devil'. They don't understand why the Lord is not using them in that manner, especially after a series of fasting or because they fasted 100 days with little or no expected results. They become jealous, disgruntled and a busy body, attacking other men of God with scandalous statements. This way, they 'kill' by mouth.

Also, Joseph's brothers could not understand why they should bow to him according to his dreams. He was the second to the last child of the family of Jacob. It did not make sense to them, so they plotted to do away with him for his dreams to be stopped from coming to pass. They felt it was an insult and damaging to their ego that the older should bow to the younger. Why should they bow to him? they thought and conspired. Why was Reuben, the first-born, not the chosen one? They would not have had a problem with that because it was customary for the younger to obey and look up to the older. They could not wrap their minds around the fact that they had to serve their younger brother. So they thought killing him was the solution to avoiding them serving Joseph, who later went on to become the prince of Egypt.

Chapter Three

The battle of the mind

Many battles go on in the mind – the mind is located in the soul – the soul is made up of your emotions, will-power, mind and conscious. The questions of Life go on in the mind, so the question of 'Why is it not me?' goes on in the mind.

You cannot see your mind; no one can see your mind – it is very private – it can think or imagine whatever it wants to at any time.

Every action starts with a thought, which is the product of the mind; people execute and act in their mind before its manifestation.

In your mind, you can be the best dancer in the world. In your mind, you can fly an aeroplane. You can be anything. The mind is always busy, back and forth. With the mind, there is no barrier, no distance and no limitation.

Believers go through the question of 'Why is it not me?' in their minds. It is part of the battle of the mind. They can't tell anyone because they are scared of the outcome, how they will be viewed, analysed and concluded upon.

"come to me all you who labor and are heavy laden and I will give you rest, take my yoke upon you and learn from me for I am gentle and lowly in heart and you will find rest for your soul." (Matthew 11:28-29)

The Devil is targetting your soul: he is interested in your rest; he is interested in your peace. He knows if he attacks your mind, it affects everything about you. Life becomes meaningless, hopeless, worthless, and you lose your joy which is your strength when you give in to the pressures of the flesh and Satan.

The Bible says that:

he that compares himself with others is not wise **(2 Corinthians 10:12)**.

Furthermore, Jesus said,

you should come to him, he will give you rest, **(Matthew 11:28)**. let your focus be about him. Seek first the kingdom of God and his righteousness and every other thing shall be added to you **(Matthew 6:33)**.

True peace and rest comes only from God.

Chapter Four

Are you going through the battles of the mind? **Do not forget that:**

The race is no longer to the swift or the battle to the strong, **(Ecclesiastes 9:11),**

it is God who favours and blesses the works of our hands. Grace qualifies the unqualified. It is not about how fast or intelligent you are; it is not about your background, your age, or your past.

When God decides to favour a man, the dumbest in the class can become the prime minister of a country. When God favours a woman, everything she touches becomes better than gold. When God favours a man, men have no choice but to honour him; men have no choice but to celebrate him.

A man receives nothing except it has been given from above **(John 3:27)**.

God is still in the business of taking people from the rubbish bin and using them to showcase his glory. Although we know the rabbit to be faster in motion than the turtle, the turtle won the race against the rabbit by wisdom and favour.

Do not forget

There is time and season for everything under the earth **(Ecclesiastes 3:1)**.

When your time comes, everything falls in place. Things you struggled with in the past becomes so easy. I later got admission into the university after four years of writing exams and trying. In the first exam I sat, I scored 240, which could not get me into the university. In the second exam, I scored 241. On the final exam, I scored 280 – the highest score in the country in that year's exam was 315. So, I was one of the highest. I did not have to know anyone to get admission.

When I told people my score, they would scream! – they did not know I had tried three times. They did not know my process. Someone else would have said 'Why?' to my score, 'Why not me?'"

My time had come, and there was no stopping me.

Do not forget

"and he said to Moses, I will have mercy on whomever I will have mercy and I will have compassion on whomever I will have compassion" (Romans 9:15)

God's ways are not our ways, neither are his thoughts our thoughts. He is sovereign; he has it all figured out. He will bless whomever he chooses to bless. He will give his gift to whomever he chooses to give. He knows and understands us more than we know and understand ourselves. He knows and understands our intentions. He knows the end from the beginning: He created us.

He said he would make Abraham the father of many nations; he had the capacity to make it happen immediately, but it took twenty-five years for Abraham to have a son in his old age. God still made him the father of many nations as he promised.

We can not question him. He is the almighty, God by himself, the all-knowing.

Chapter Five

What to do

Rejoice with those who rejoice and weep with those who weep (**Romans 12:15**).

Be genuinely happy for the success of another, you can not attract what you attack.

Celebrate those who have what you desire. Appreciate them. Walk up to them and ask questions if you are not sure how to get there – they may tell you one or two things that will help. Stop attacking them. Stop spreading rumours about them: you are not their God.

If God decides to bless a man, no one can curse him. You can not bring down a man that God himself raised. Attacking them in any form will never make you feel better; it can only make you feel worse. My principal once said:

"If you like what someone is doing or what they are wearing, walk up to them and tell them how much you appreciate what they are doing or how beautiful they look. It will make you feel good instead of being jealous. Celebrate someone whose season has come, do not kill yourself over what you do not have now. Your time will come."

Blessing by association

God blessed the house of Potiphar because of Joseph. Because Joseph was in the house of Potiphar, Potiphar's household prospered. There is a blessing that rubs-off on you as a result of your association with someone. If you are a friend to a millionaire, you will definitely befit no matter how stingy he may be. That is why the bible says in (**2 Corinthians 6: 14**)

"do not be unequally yoked together with unbelievers",

because when destructions come in their midst, it may affect you also. When we associate with people, we contact something. When you desire what someone has, associate with them instead of killing yourself over nothing.

Believe God for yours and be patient with him, knowing that, if it is *his* will, it will come to pass. **(1 John 5: 14)** says:

If we ask anything according to his will, he hears us.

Yours will definitely come.

About the Author

Olamma Maji, a graduate of Mass Communication, came to Western Australia from Nigeria A mother of three beautiful children and wife to Apostle Isaiah Maji, founder of JPPM, Olamma wrote this book to encourage everyone to understand that there is a time for everything under the sun and everyone's destiny sometimes defers.

www.ingramcontent.com/pod-product-compliance
Lightning Source LLC
Chambersburg PA
CBHW071551080526
44588CB00011B/1866